Simply Classical

23 Well Known Masterpieces

Arranged by Mary K. Sallee

Simply Classical is a collection of arias, rondos, sonatina movements, string quartet movements, symphonic themes, and other famous works from the Classical period of music history (ca. 1750–1820). These selections have been carefully arranged by Mary K. Sallee for Easy Piano, making them accessible to pianists of all ages. Phrase markings, fingering, pedaling and dynamics have been included to aid with interpretation, and a large print size makes the notation easy to read.

The Classical period has a diverse and exciting body of music. Some of the world's most beloved melodies come from this era. Franz Joseph Haydn's *"Surprise" Symphony* contains one of the most famous musical jokes ever written. Wolfgang Amadeus Mozart's *Eine kleine Nachtmusik* highlights Classical form and balance. Ludwig van Beethoven's *Für Elise* is one of the most popular pieces for piano students. Classical period music can be solemn and stately as in Haydn's *"Kaiser" String Quartet*, one of his most ambitious chamber works written around the same time as his famous oratorio *The Creation*. Classical period music can also be energetic and insistent as in Beethoven's *Rondo a capriccio* ("Rage over a Lost Penny"), an incomplete piano piece that Beethoven composed in his youth, which was published posthumously after having been completed by Anton Diabelli. With its ability to evoke thoughts of nobility and courtly grace, and with its magical proportions of melody, harmony, and form, this music has been embraced by musicians and audiences, young and old, around the world. For these reasons and more, the Classical selections on the following pages are exciting to explore.

After all, this is *Simply Classical!*

Contents

Ecossaise

(from *The Ruins of Athens*)

Ludwig van Beethoven
Arranged by Mary K. Sallee

Light and animated

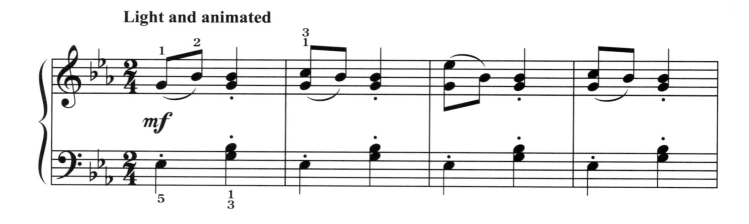

LH marcato
to the end

Für Elise

Ludwig van Beethoven
Arranged by Mary K. Sallee

With motion

German Dance
(from *Twelve German Dances*, WoO 13)

Ludwig van Beethoven
Arranged by Mary K. Sallee

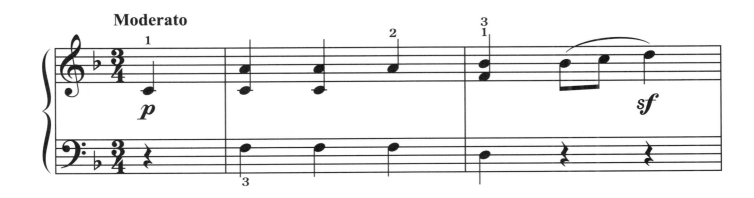

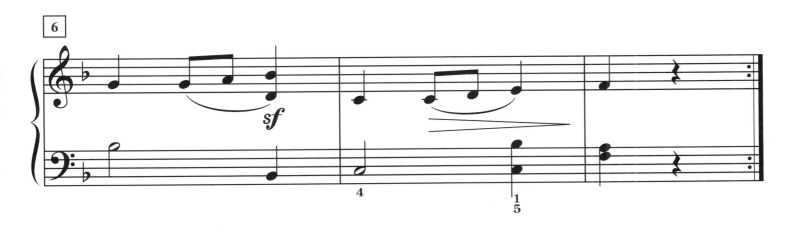

12

Minuet in G Major

Ludwig van Beethoven
Arranged by Mary K. Sallee

"Moonlight" Sonata

Ludwig van Beethoven
Arranged by Mary K. Sallee

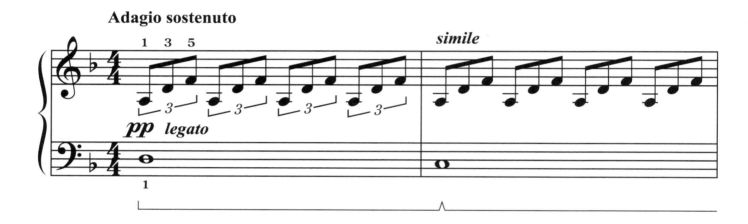

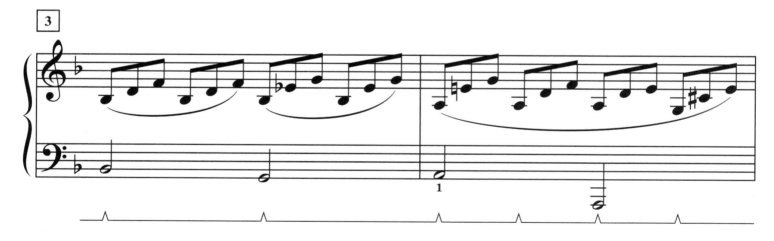

Ode to Joy

(from *Symphony No. 9*)

Ludwig van Beethoven
Arranged by Mary K. Sallee

(a) The RH in m. 17 (and similarly in mm. 25–27, and 38) may be played:

Rondo a capriccio

("The Rage over a Lost Penny")

Ludwig van Beethoven
Arranged by Mary K. Sallee

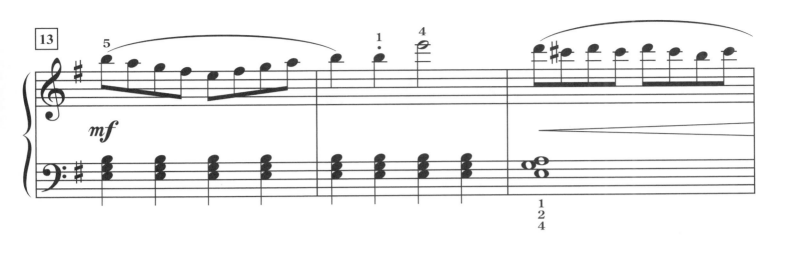

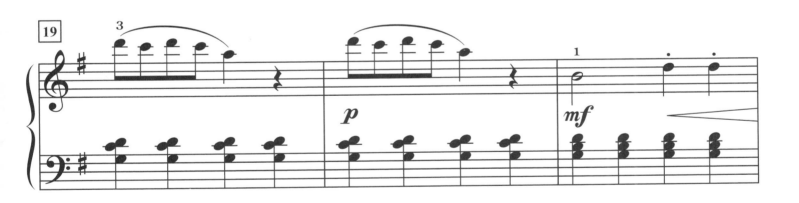

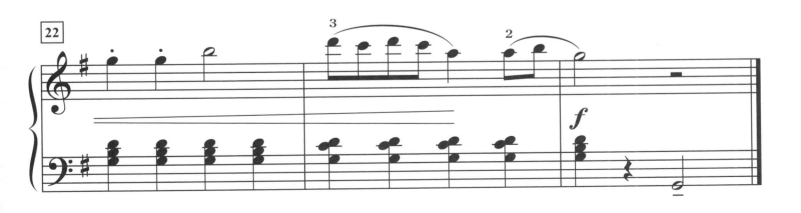

Turkish March

(from *The Ruins of Athens*)

Ludwig van Beethoven
Arranged by Mary K. Sallee

Variations on a Theme from the "Eroica" Symphony

Ludwig van Beethoven
Arranged by Mary K. Sallee

Quickly

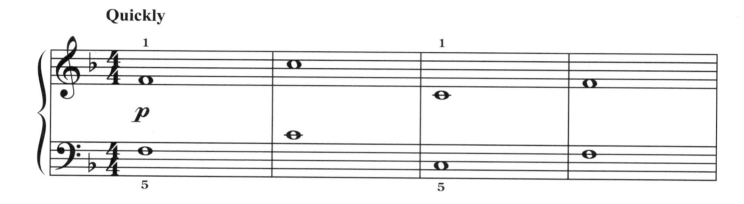

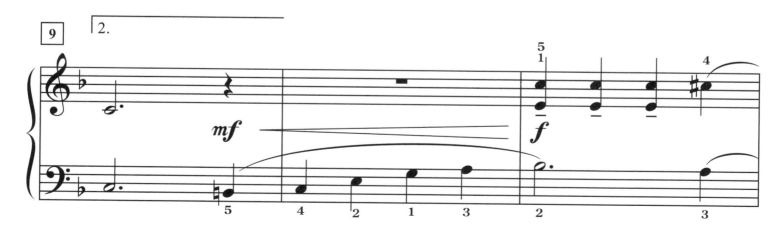

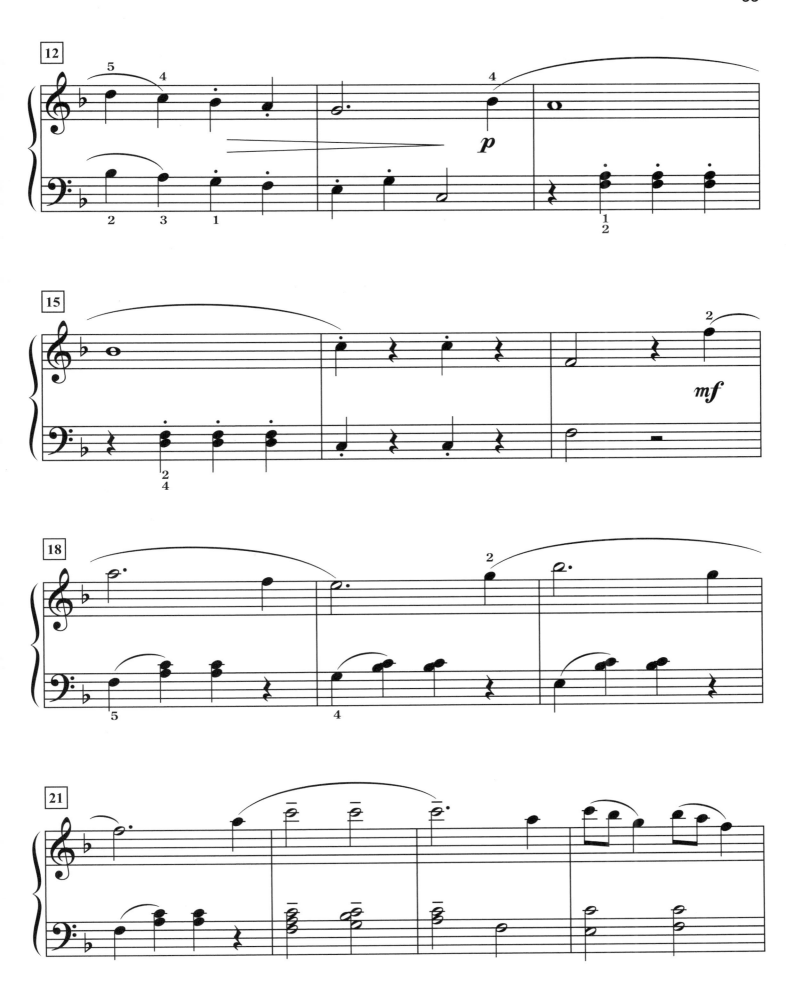

Theme from the "Pastoral" Symphony

Ludwig van Beethoven
Arranged by Mary K. Sallee

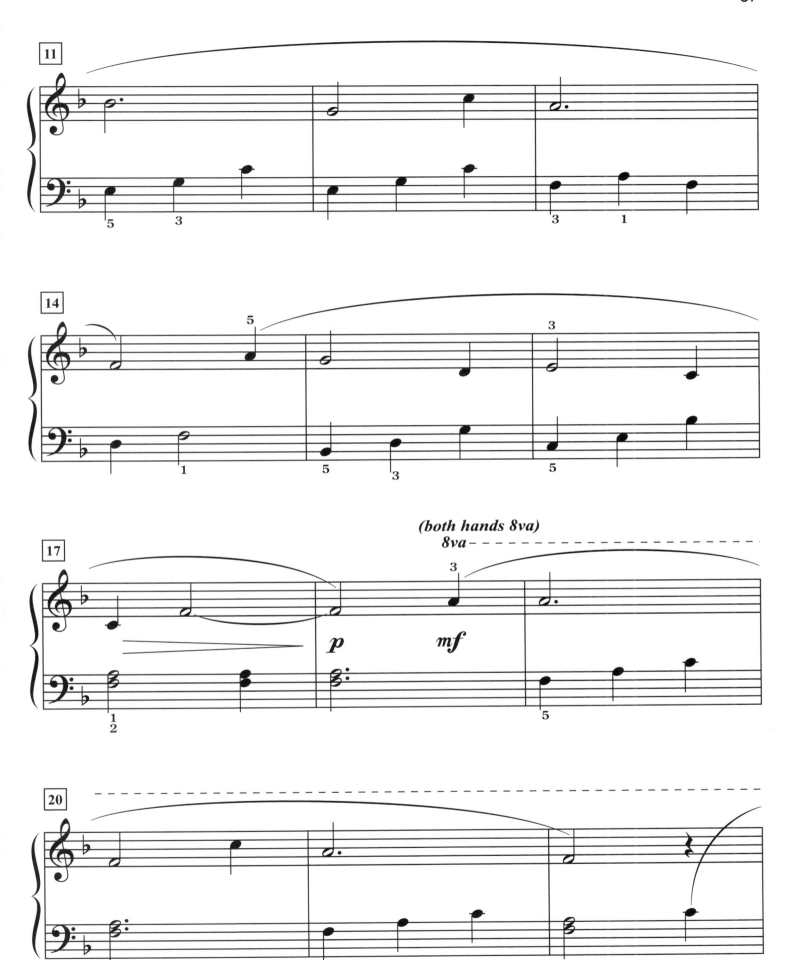

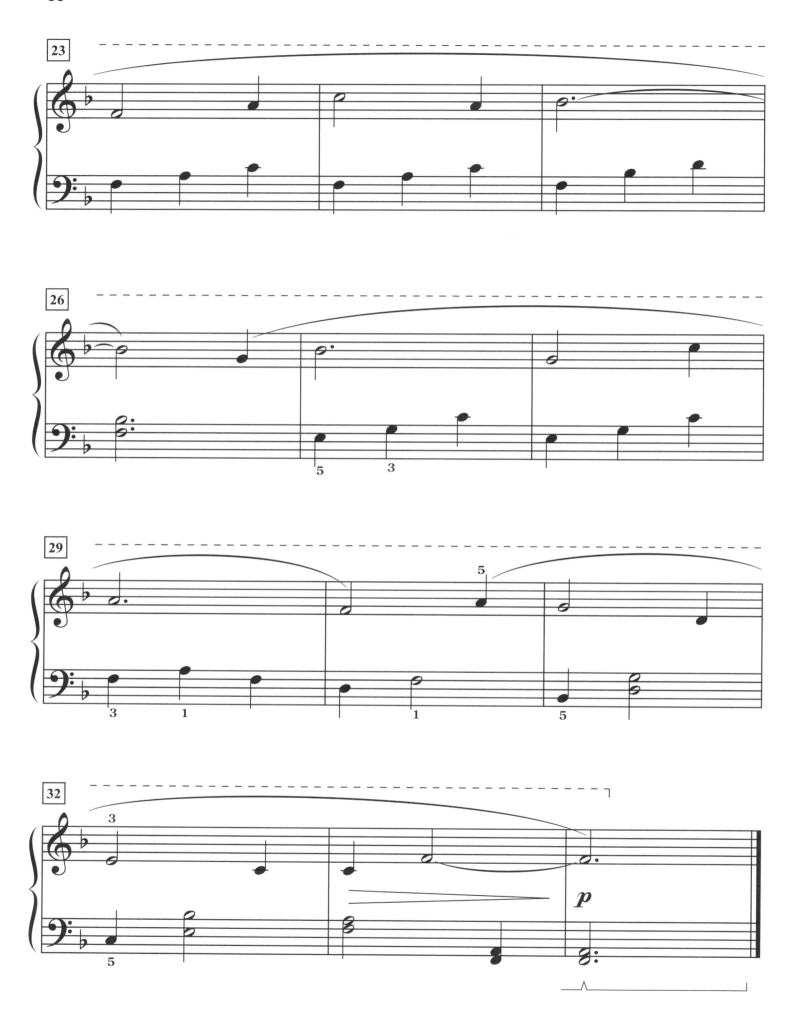

Sonatina No. 1

(Allegro)

(from *Six Sonatinas*, Op. 36)

Muzio Clementi
Arranged by Mary K. Sallee

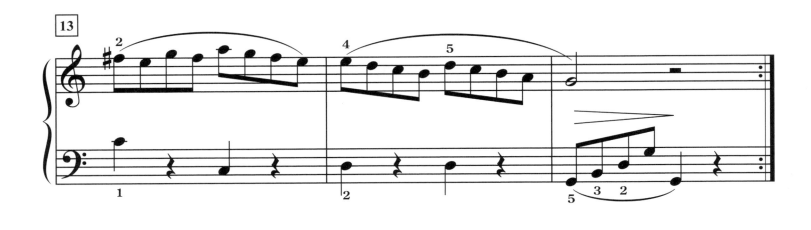

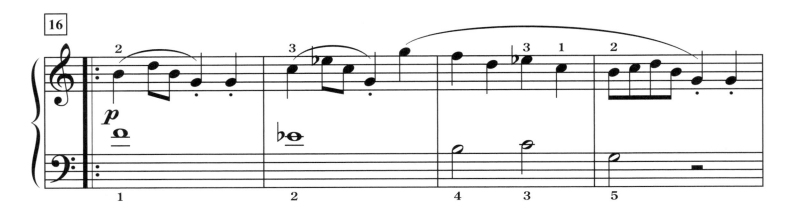

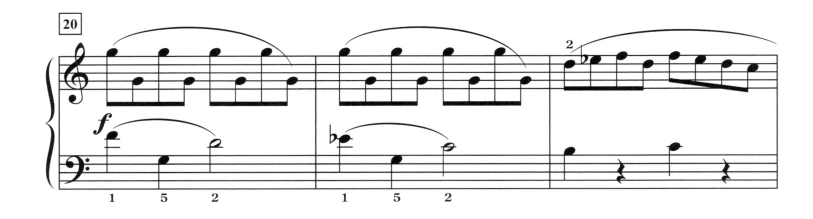

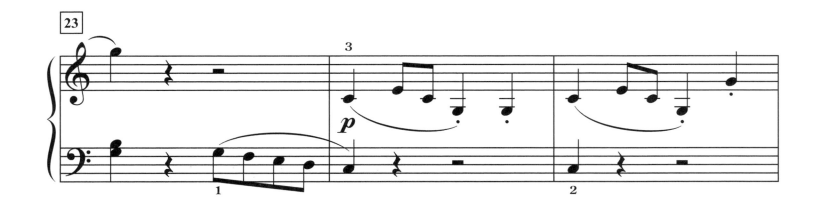

41

Sonatina No. 1
(Andante)
(from *Six Sonatinas*, Op. 36)

Muzio Clementi
Arranged by Mary K. Sallee

44

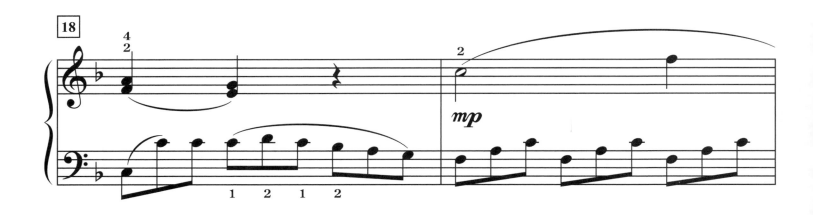

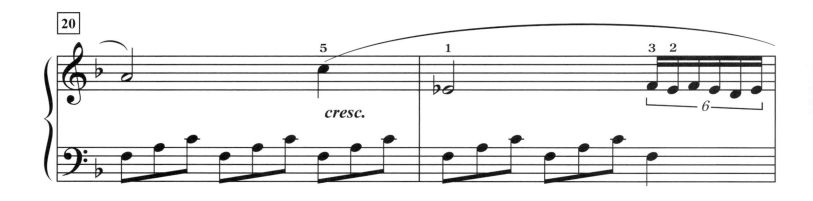

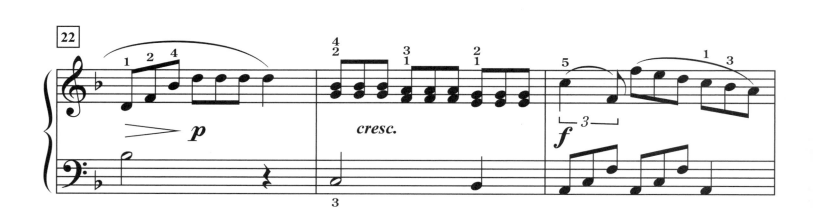

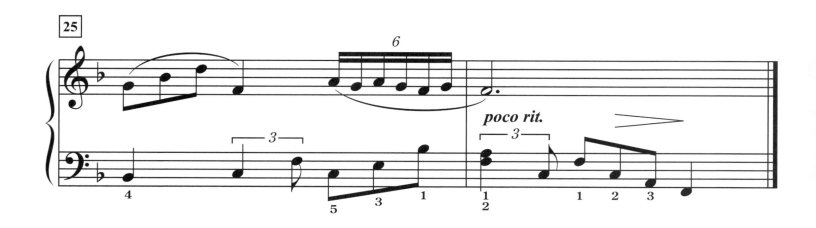

Gypsy Rondo

Franz Joseph Haydn
Arranged by Mary K. Sallee

Quickly, in two

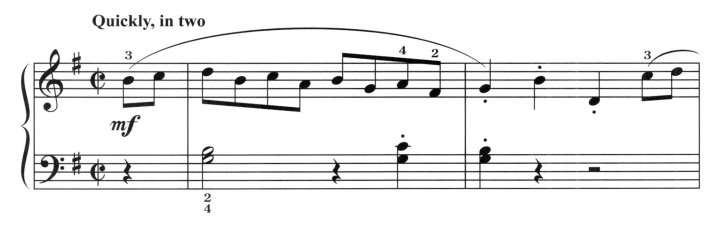

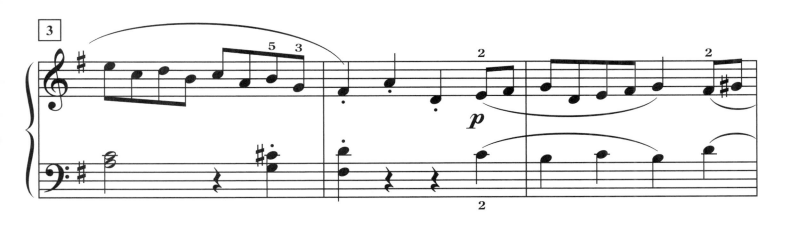

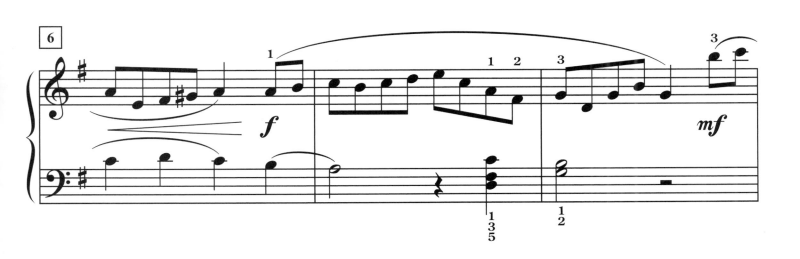

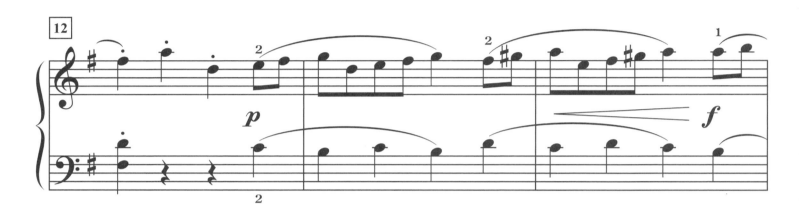

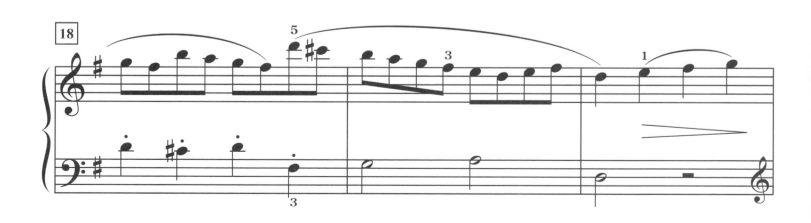

47

Theme from the "Kaiser" String Quartet

Franz Joseph Haydn
Arranged by Mary K. Sallee

Adagio cantabile

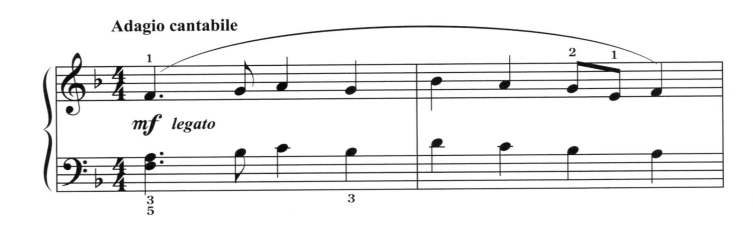

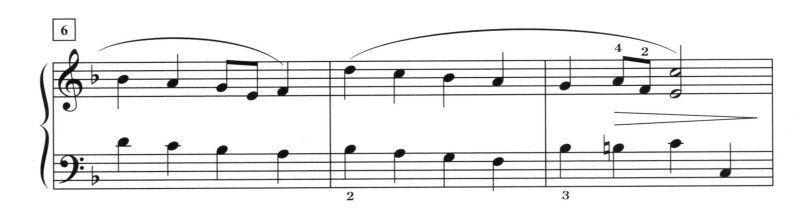

Theme from the "London" Symphony

Franz Joseph Haydn
Arranged by Mary K. Sallee

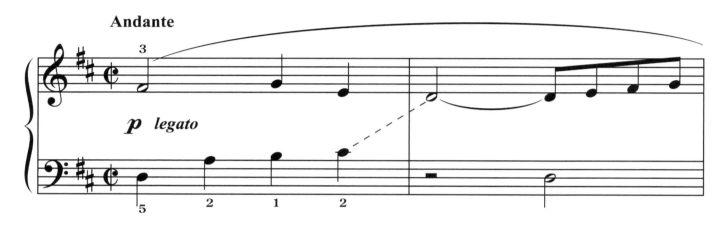

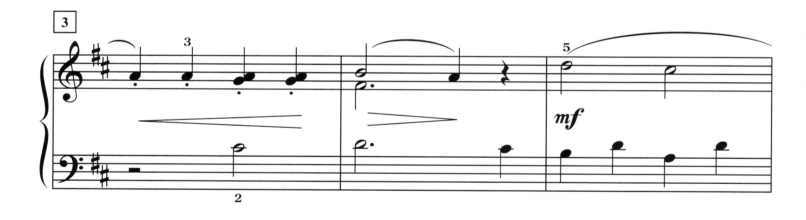

Theme from the "Surprise" Symphony

Franz Joseph Haydn
Arranged by Mary K. Sallee

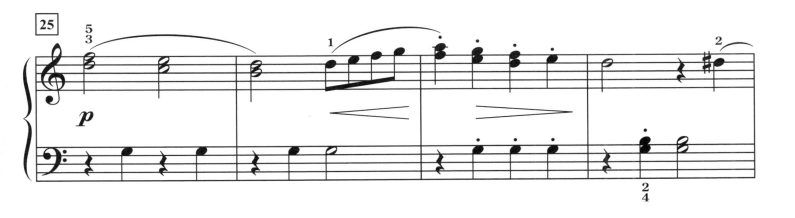

Theme from the Cello Concerto
in D Major

Franz Joseph Haydn
Arranged by Mary K. Sallee

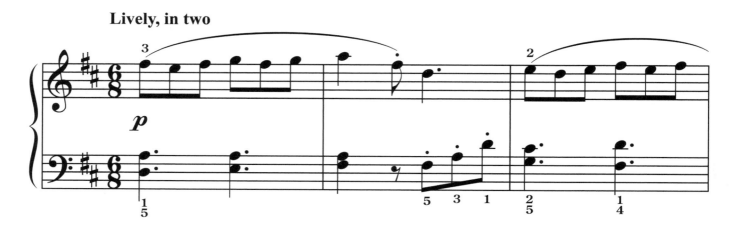

Eine kleine Nachtmusik

(Allegro)

Wolfgang Amadeus Mozart
Arranged by Mary K. Sallee

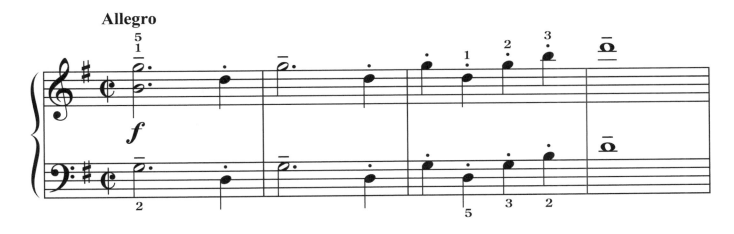

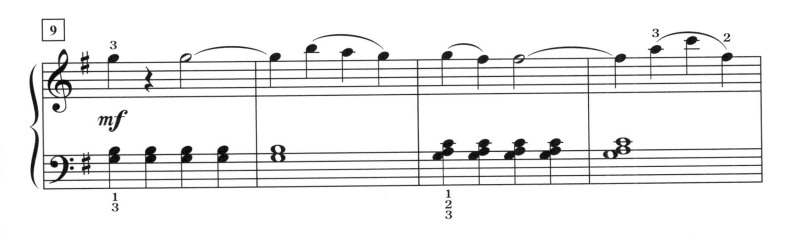

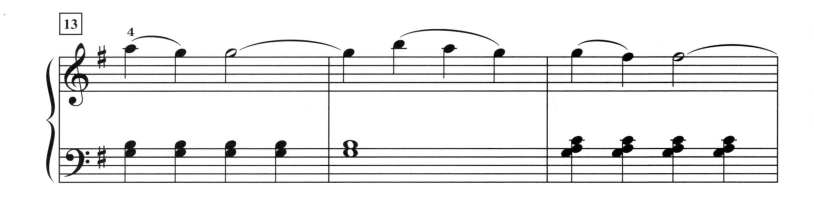

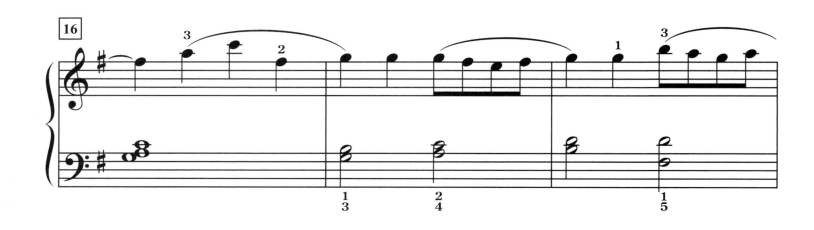

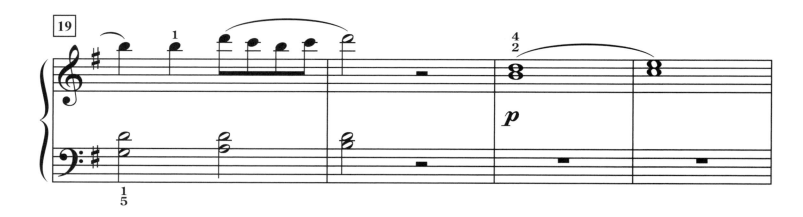

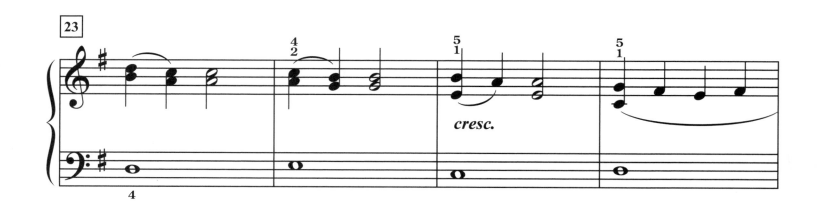

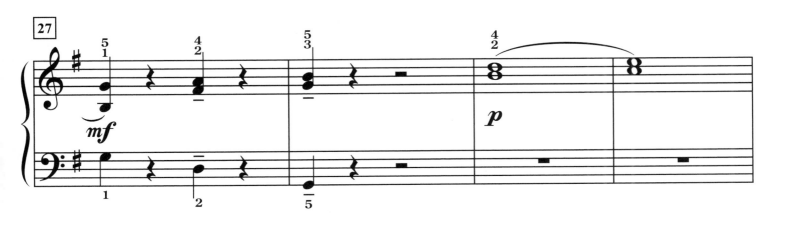

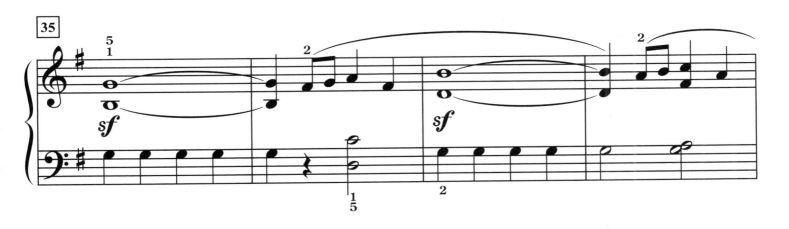

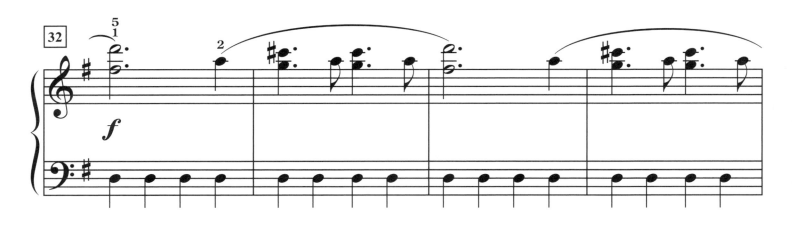

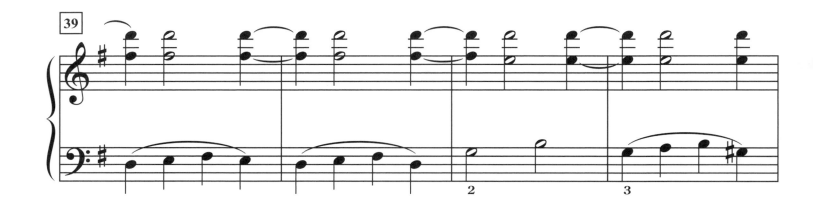

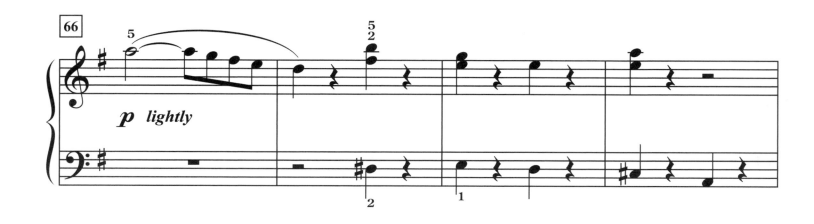

Ein Mädchen oder Weibchen

(from *The Magic Flute*)

Wolfgang Amadeus Mozart
Arranged by Mary K. Sallee

Stately, but light

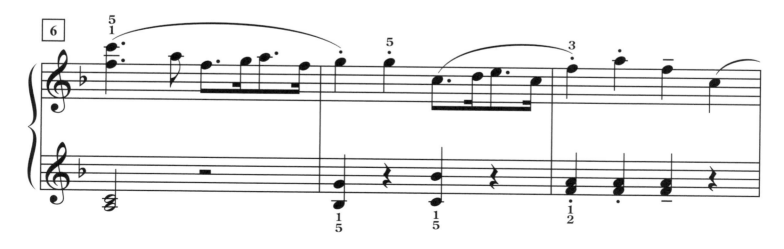

Là ci darem la mano

(from *Don Giovanni*)

Wolfgang Amadeus Mozart
Arranged by Mary K. Sallee

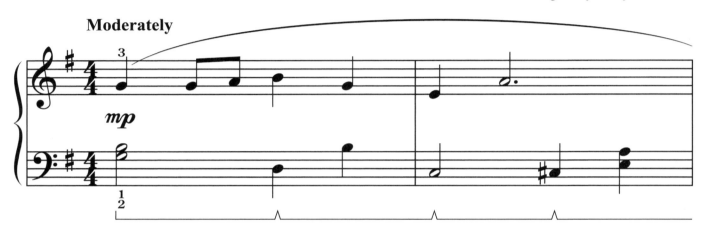

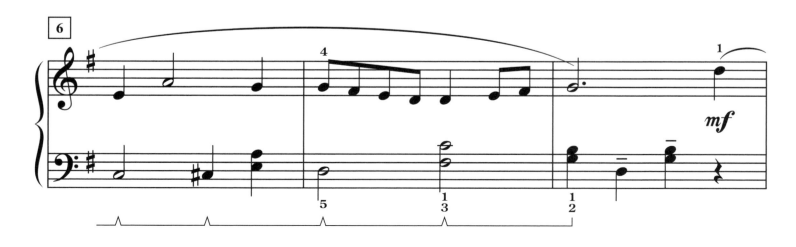

67

69

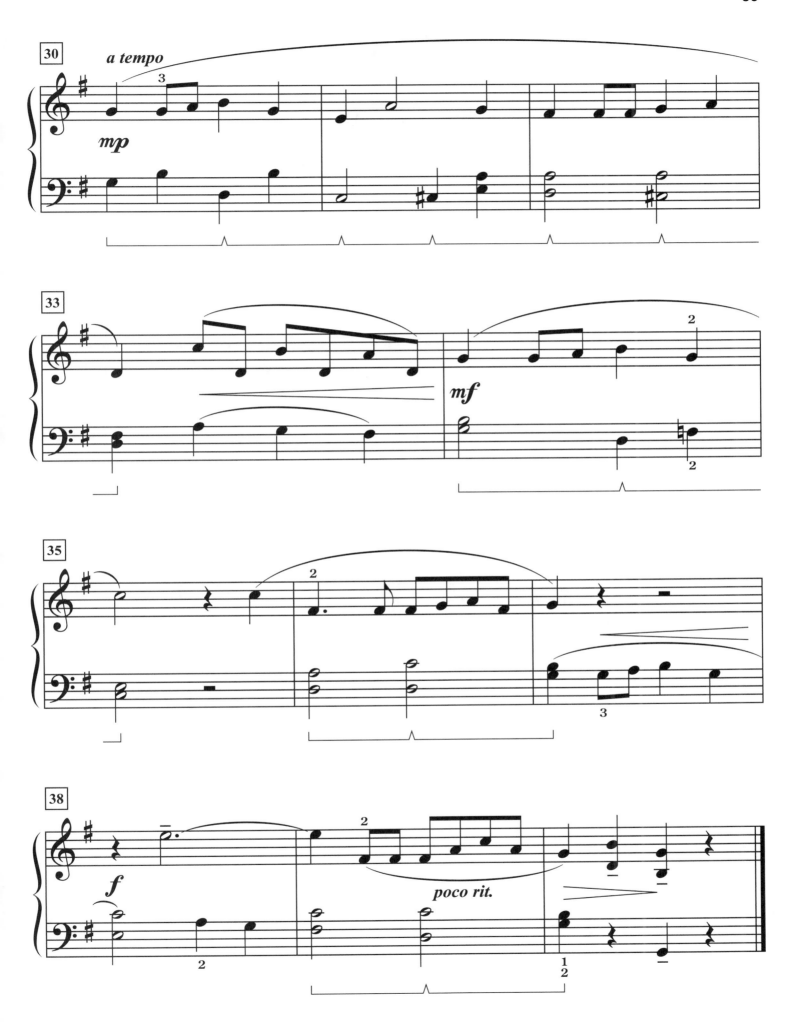

Menuetto

(from *Don Giovanni*)

Wolfgang Amadeus Mozart
Arranged by Mary K. Sallee

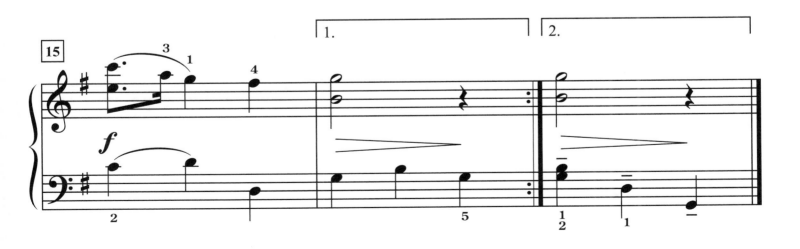

Rondo alla Turca

(from *Sonata No. 11*, K. 331)

Wolfgang Amadeus Mozart
Arranged by Mary K. Sallee

With haste, in two

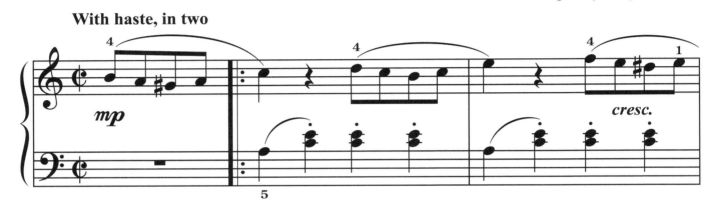

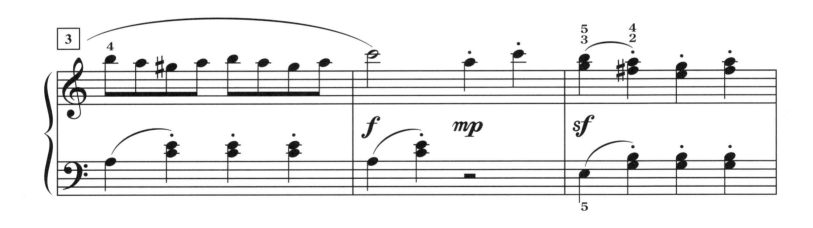

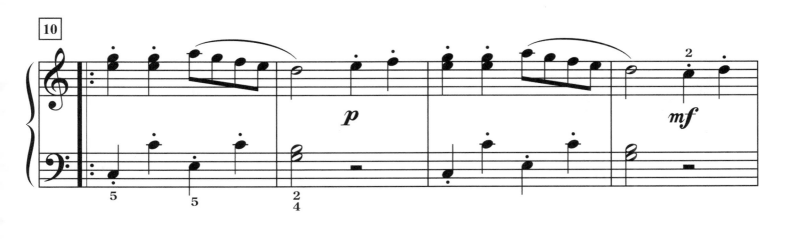

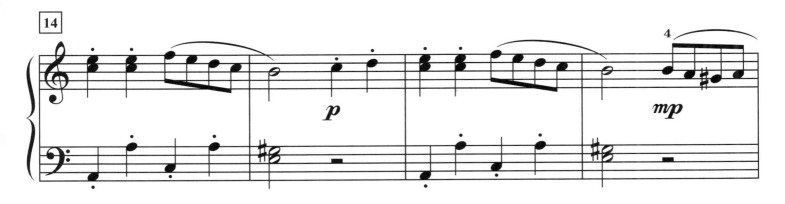

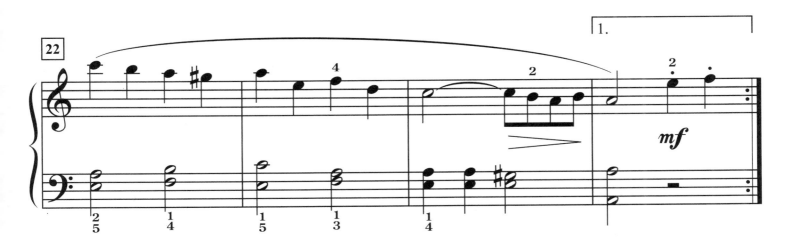

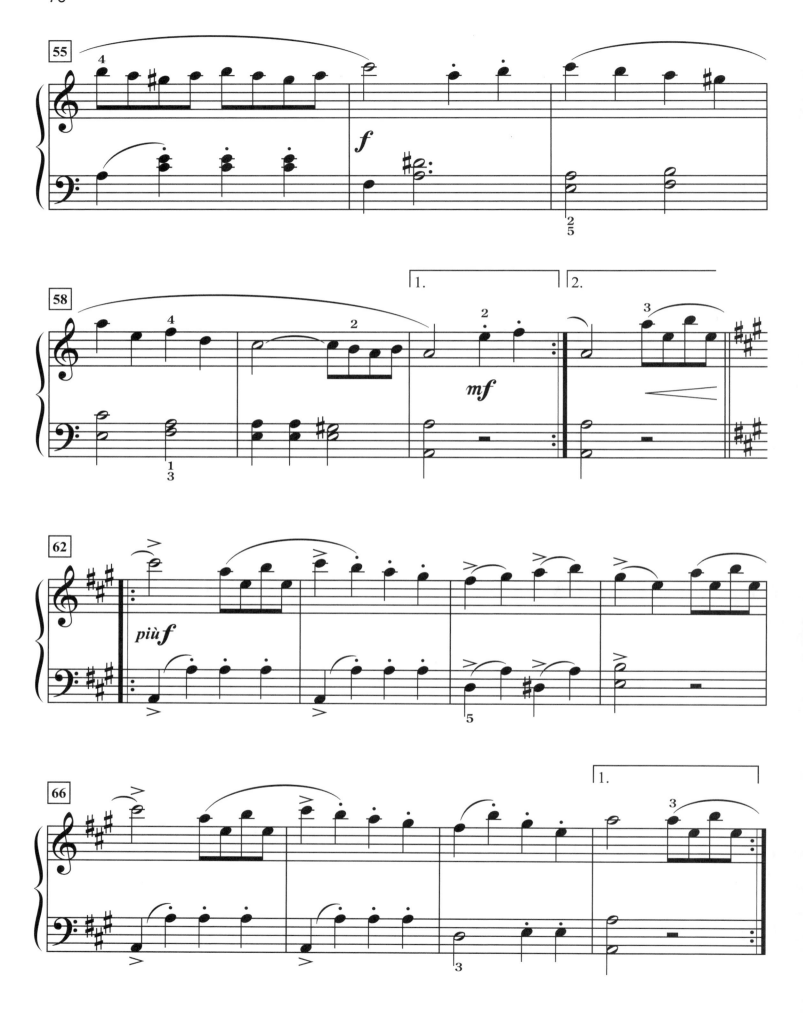

Laudate Dominum

(from *Vesperae solennes de confessore*)

Wolfgang Amadeus Mozart
Arranged by Mary K. Sallee